THE ART
OF
MAKING TEA

An Album of Recipes, Portraits,
and Other Rituals

by

Elizabeth Jones Hanley

Elizabeth Jones Hanley (signature)

THE MID-AMERICA PRESS, INC.
Warrensburg, Missouri 64093-0575

Acknowledgements

These poems, in earlier versions, first appeared in
Capper's: "Baking Day," "Grandma Makes Plum
Jelly."

FIRST EDITION

ISBN 0-910479-04-6

Financial assistance for this project has been provided by the Missouri
Arts Council, a state agency.

A Missouri Poets Chapbook

The Art of Making Tea

*An Album of Recipes, Portraits,
and Other Rituals*

by

Elizabeth Jones Hanley

The Mid-America Press, Inc.,
Poetry Chapbooks Series

CONTENTS

"nobody, not even the rain, has such small hands"
　　　　　　　　—e.e. cummings

FOR KATE

Soft rain beyond the window
dims the warm room.
Your once-bright flower face has faded
petal by petal.
I watch you open and close
on the world,
you do not know me anymore.
One day perhaps I'll be where you are now:
reaching my hand toward a stranger
who used to be family.
The rain falls between us.
Such small hands.

GRANDMA MAKES PLUM JELLY

Hours in the kitchen:
pitting, cooking, canning.
Half a jar
gone by the end of breakfast
with all the family
at the table.
"Eat up, there's plenty more."

Every summer, every breakfast:
pitting, cooking, canning.
She sent us home at end of summer
with jelly newly made.
"Eat up, there's plenty more."

Years in the kitchen:
pitting, cooking, canning.
Breakfast now is over.
I have one last jar
to taste of summer.
Grandma doesn't make her jelly anymore.

AUTUMN

Slashed with rain,
the leaves turn
brass red and yellow
against the gray clouds.
Cool wind.
The chimes
outside my window
tell me winter
is drawing near.

APPLE-PICKING

The sign reads, "Pick your own."
But "You're too little," Mom tells me.
My brother, in the top of the tree,
tosses ripe, red ones
down to waiting hands
and paper bags.
The wind chilly through my sweater,
sunshine warm on my face.
I throw back my arms, close my eyes
and spin—the world still turning—
until I find myself
lying on soft grass,
musty smell of apples in my nose.
This must be what it's like
to climb through the branches and sway
at the top of the world.

GARDEN PARTY

The hedge grows thick
at the bottom of the garden,
presses close against the woods.
In the sleepy afternoon
the sun pierces through the gloom:
then the toadstools come alive.
They bloom forth in shafts of light,
dance among the flowers.
The magical people.
They ring the bluebells,
swing from daffodils,
snap at the dragons' teeth,
their voices like birdsong.
The sun moves on,
the hedge is thick with gloom.
Just toadstools
at the bottom of the garden.

HAY STONES

These hay stacks
are standing stones.
>>Dance among them!
>>They are here today.
Gray sky low,
they dot green field.
>>Dance among them!
>>*They will not stay.*

MEETING IN THE OLD CEMETERY

Red hooded jacket, picnic basket,
I step into that other world
of gnarled trees
and last year's leaves.
No birds, no squirrels.
Even the sun turns dark
within the wrought-iron fence.
Surrounded by stone,
chill in my bones,
fingers trace worn carved words.
Shadows lengthen.

AUCTION BARN

The old, iron fence
leans on the barn:
History in rusty sections.
We find the gate, step into
long thin aisles of memories.

A horse cart with shafts
drives us backward.
Dry, rough wood.

Chairs here and there,
the squeak of legs pushed
along the floor after dinner.
Click of knitting needles,
rattle of cups.
A soda fountain bar
in several pieces.
"All in working order."

Rain outside
echoes in the space.
"Need an ancestor?"
My mother holds up a portrait.
I look at the pale, nondescript face:
The Ancestor.
Father, cousin, uncle
to the people whose voices
echo in this space,
to the child babbling outside,
to us
standing here by an old wicker table
next to a doll's highchair.

PERSPECTIVE

Old Man Ferguson.
All afternoon
he sits on the park bench.
Anyone who passes by he tells—
lives he has not led,
places he has not been to,
a person he never was.
Until he hears himself.

A hawk skims low over the lake
wing tips dip in the water.
Old Man Ferguson walks slowly home.

TOO LATE

Italian Cream Cake—
three layers—
Did you remember the plates?
cream cheese icing
with nuts—
What about the napkins?
carried, oh so gently,
nestled in in the box,
ready for the reunion—
Don't forget the forks.
and placed on the roof of the car.
"I think that's everything. Off at last!"
. . . where did you put the cake?

QUESTING THE SUN

On the hill north of town,
a fire truck slowly decays
in the sun.
I imagine it long ago, when
it wailed down the street—
armored
Arthurian red.
Richard Harris wheels no longer turn.
A hollow crown,
it rests
quiet in the sun
on a hill where cows graze.

TOUCHSTONES

Winter afternoon,
cold, shallow sky.
The field brown and white with snow.
Discordant cry and flap of wings.
Taste of north wind in my mouth.
Woodsmoke on the air.
A church bell tolls.

WINTER

This is the quiet time.
Stars spark in the sky.
Another season's turning.
An early snow this year.
A hard winter to come.

IT SNOWED LAST NIGHT

Not much. Just enough
to touch the rooftops,
gather into corners,
and kiss the brick sidewalk
in front of the house.

BAKING DAY

On a snowy afternoon,
homemade bread.
Nothing tastes as good—
crusty
dripping butter
oven-warm—
a hard day of work.

THE SAXOPHONE

The girl
plays a saxophone.
She is small
and thin.
Long, brown hair falls
down her back.
She sways with an easy rhythm.
And the saxophone is gold
with an oval-framed iris
embossed on the side.
"It belonged," she says, "to my grandmother."

WATCHING

The woman in black sits,
patient eyes,
face pleated with lines,
hands folded
in her lap.
She looks out the window,
watches the street,
the traffic,
the lives of others—
no movement but the slow rise and fall
of her breast,
and her eyes
gently closing.

SUMMER

Warm, bright afternoon,
smell of water and earth:
a heady aroma.
The brook whispers
in the shade.
This branch a perfect fit.
I lean back and close my eyes,
listen to what the brook has to say.

THE GENTLE DAYS

In a stack of handkerchiefs
messy in the basket on the dresser:
one white, starched, lace-edged,
neatly folded.
Fingers smooth the material
and the scent of perfume rises
faded and sweet
like a sepia photograph.

ITALIAN CUISINE

Antonio's clam spaghetti
with chilled white wine.
A meticulously tossed salad.
Italian music softly plays
romantic—quickening beat.
The young couple sit in a cozy corner.
Her hair glows in candle light,
his face shines, dark skin touched warm red.
She murmurs something, soft.
He responds, flash of teeth.
They look at their plates,
at each other,
their plates.
He sips his wine
and she twirls her linguini
around and around with her fork.

SCONES

2 cups flour,
½ teaspoon salt,
2 ½ teaspoons baking powder
¼ cup sugar.

Ingredients shift and slide together:
>   *errands run,*
>   *daily chores*
>   *blend into one.*

Cut in 1/3 cup butter.

>   *Coming together at end of day,*
>   *dinner around the table.*

1 egg
and enough milk for a total of 2/3 cup liquid.
Fold together, knead and roll.
Cut into rounds and place on a cookie sheet.
>   *Would that everything*
>   *mixed together and baked*
>   *for 12-15 minutes at 425*
>   *came out so well.*

CHRISTMAS DRESS

Granny peeked from around the door,
sashayed across the floor—
"Do you think it's all right? Do you think it will do?"—
stood among debris
of Christmas paper so all could see:
New blue dress, tag hanging down,
pink, fuzzy slippers on her feet,
all dressed up and ready for town.
She twirled in a circle ever so neat.
"Do you think it's all right? Do you think it will do?"

"I MEANT TO DO THAT"

Asleep on the edge of the couch
she stirs,
stretches, turns, slips,
tumbles sideways
to land
with an acrobat twist
four feet down
on the floor
looks around,
without comment—
avoiding my eye—
straightens her tail
and stalks out the door.

HOME OWNERS

These women
in their afternoon tea dresses
stand on the porch
and in the yard.
Solemn faces
for formal occasions,
like picture taking
and tea
and afternoon tea dresses.

DREAMS

The woman moves the cloth
carefully among the china figures,
once a month, for years.
The rag flutters like a gray moth,

lands delicately on each piece.
Dust swirls around the woman's face,
glitters brightly in the sun.
Half-remembered dreams.

The woman sighs, moves the cloth
carefully among the china figures.
The rag flutters like a gray moth.
Dreams settle back down to dust.

GHOSTS

crouch at the foot of the bed,
duck beneath the stair,
slip into shadow.
The voices echo around us.
I hear them whisper my name.

GHOST IN THE KALEIDOSCOPE

I see her dancing there
(colors shift within the light),
bright flowers in her hair.

Who is she? Take heed, beware.
Unbidden to my sight,
I see me dancing there.

And now the dance has stopped (how rare
to see those colored facets bright),
such bright flowers in her hair—

I cannot see this dance we share.
Then patterns dazzle with such light
I find us dancing where

this world drifts, lost, in starless air.
And then the pattern—dark and light.
I see her dancing there,
bright flowers in her hair.

DREAM CATCHER

Spider weaves her web:
dreams spun in the dark.
Bad dreams she captures, wraps them well.
Good dreams she lets through.
Morning, sun-glistened with dew,
they sparkle:
dreams, imaginings, truths.
Patient, spider waits,
weaves her web.

HABITS

I hear you
even though I know you're gone—
know it to be true.

A shadow comes into my view
each afternoon across the lawn.
I know I hear you,

hear a voice that once I knew
sing an old familiar song—
although you're gone. It's true:

each afternoon I wait for you.
Even though I know I'm wrong,
I still hear you

coming home, still wait for you.
I hear your steps upon
the porch—but it's not you.
Knowing that it's true.

MENDING OLD LACE

The straight-back chair
hard against her spine,
crochet hook in hand.
The lace, worn and thin,
a cobweb strand of memories,
of dreams.
She mends old lace—
sees the past in
soft and pliant fragments,
weaves the past together.

THE ART OF MAKING TEA

She is well-versed in the art.
       Fresh water to boil
       and heat the pot
Grace and form in each movement,
no rush.
       2 bags, steep a full 5 minutes
       This last part is essential.
A ceremony performed just so,
a balm to sooth mind and soul.
       A pinch of sugar
       then the milk swirls and mixes.
Like a dance.

Elizabeth Jones Hanley

Elizabeth Jones Hanley is a Missouri poet whose works have appeared in *Capper's*, *Standard*, and *The Witness*. A former librarian, she currently participates in workshops for elementary schools and Young Author's Conferences. Her most recent project is *The Well, the Witch and the Ring*, a juvenile fiction novel told in a series of poems.